FIREFLIES

by Liza Jacobs

BLACKBIRCH®
PRESS

San Diego • Detroit • New York • San Francisco • Cleveland • New Haven, Conn. • Waterville, Maine • London • Munich

© 2003 by Blackbirch Press™. Blackbirch Press™ is an imprint of The Gale Group, Inc., a division of Thomson Learning, Inc.

Blackbirch Press™ and Thomson Learning™ are trademarks used herein under license.

For more information, contact
The Gale Group, Inc.
27500 Drake Rd.
Farmington Hills, MI 48331-3535
Or you can visit our Internet site at http://www.gale.com

Photographs © 1999 by Chen Jen-Hsiang

Cover photograph © Corbis

© 1999 by Chin-Chin Publications Ltd.

No. 274-1, Sec.1 Ho-Ping E. Rd., Taipei, Taiwan, R.O.C.
Tel: 886-2-2363-3486 Fax: 886-2-2363-6081

LIBRARY OF CONGRESS CATALOGING-IN-PUBLICATION DATA

Jacobs, Liza.
  Fireflies / by Liza Jacobs.
     v. cm. -- (Wild wild world)
  Includes bibliographical references (p. 24).
  Contents: About fireflies -- Mating -- Four stages of growth -- Many
  kinds of fireflies.
   ISBN 1-4103-0048-X (hardback : alk. paper)
   1. Fireflies--Juvenile literature. [1. Fireflies.] I. Title. II.
  Series.

  QL596.L28J23 2003
  595.76'44--dc21

                                                         2003001468

Printed in Taiwan
10 9 8 7 6 5 4 3 2 1

Table of Contents

About Fireflies 4

Mating 6

Four Stages of Growth 8

Nighttime Creatures .10

Molting 12

Pupae 14

Into an Adult 16

Food for Others 18

Many Kinds of Fireflies 20

For More Information 24

Glossary 24

About Fireflies

A firefly is not a fly at all—it is a kind of beetle! Fireflies are also called lightning bugs. They rest and stay out of sight during the day. At night, they leave their hiding places.

Fireflies are easy to spot because they flash their glowing light in the dark! All kinds of fireflies glow when they are young. Many kinds of adult fireflies can glow, too.

A firefly's light organs are on the underside of its abdomen (rear section). When chemicals inside a firefly's body mix together, the energy makes light!

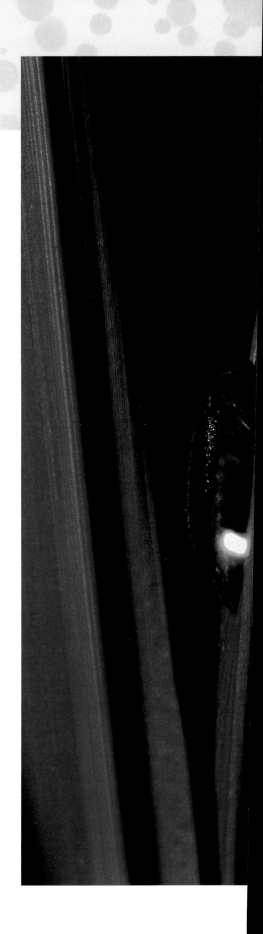

Mating

To find a mate, most male fireflies fly around blinking their lights in a certain pattern.

Females watch the signals, waiting near the ground on a leaf or plant. If a female is interested in a male, she flashes her light back until the two find each other. Mating can last several hours.

Four Stages of Growth

Like many insects, fireflies go through an amazing cycle of life. A firefly has four stages of life as it changes from egg, to larva, to pupa, and finally, to an adult firefly.

The first stage of life occurs just a few days after mating. The female firefly is ready to lay her eggs. Some kinds of fireflies lay about 40 smooth, round eggs. Other types lay hundreds. The eggs take about a month to hatch. Then the larvae wriggle out of their shells.

Nighttime Creatures

Most fireflies are nocturnal. That means they are active at night. Adult fireflies mainly drink plant nectar. They spend their nights searching for mates.

Firefly larvae come out at night to search for food. They eat slugs, earthworms, and other soft-bodied insects. They love to eat snails. Fireflies often find slugs and snails by following the trail of slime these creatures leave behind. The larvae use their strong jaws to grip an animal. Then they shoot liquid from their jaws into the animal. The liquid turns the animal's body into a soupy liquid and the larva sucks up its meal!

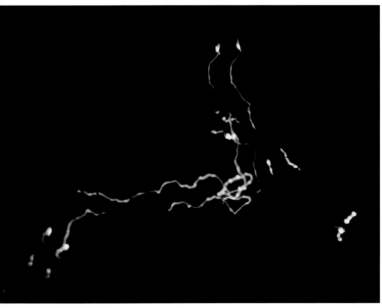

11

Molting

The more the larvae eat, the more they grow. Like other insects, fireflies have a covering over their bodies called an exoskeleton. This covering does not grow with the insect.

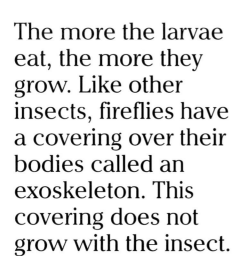  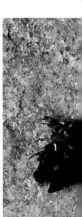

In order to reach its adult size, a firefly larva has to shed its exoskeleton. This is called molting. They shed their skin several times. Underneath the old skin, is a new one!

Pupae

When a larva has grown as much as it is going to, it is ready to become a pupa. Some fireflies attach themselves to the undersides of leaves during this stage. Others dig a shallow opening on the ground. Many fireflies dig a hole underneath the ground. Wherever it finds shelter, the larva begins to change into a pupa. In 30 to 40 days, it molts again. This time, a stiff pupa covering is under the skin.

Into an Adult

Over the next 10 days, a pupa changes into an adult. Then it molts one last time. The adult firefly is now fully formed with antennae, large eyes, and two pairs of wings. (Like other beetles, the front pair of wings is stiff and protects the back pair of flying wings.)

The firefly is ready to dig its way to the surface. Male fireflies go off in search of a mate to begin the life cycle all over again.

Food for Others

Frogs, toads, lizards, birds, and many kinds of insects eat fireflies. Spiders catch fireflies in their webs. Poisonous ants kill fireflies, and praying mantises crunch them up for lunch! Fireflies can often escape an attack by hiding or flying away.

Some male fireflies have a secret weapon. A foul-tasting poison in their bodies keeps many animals from ever trying to eat a firefly a second time!

Many Kinds of Fireflies

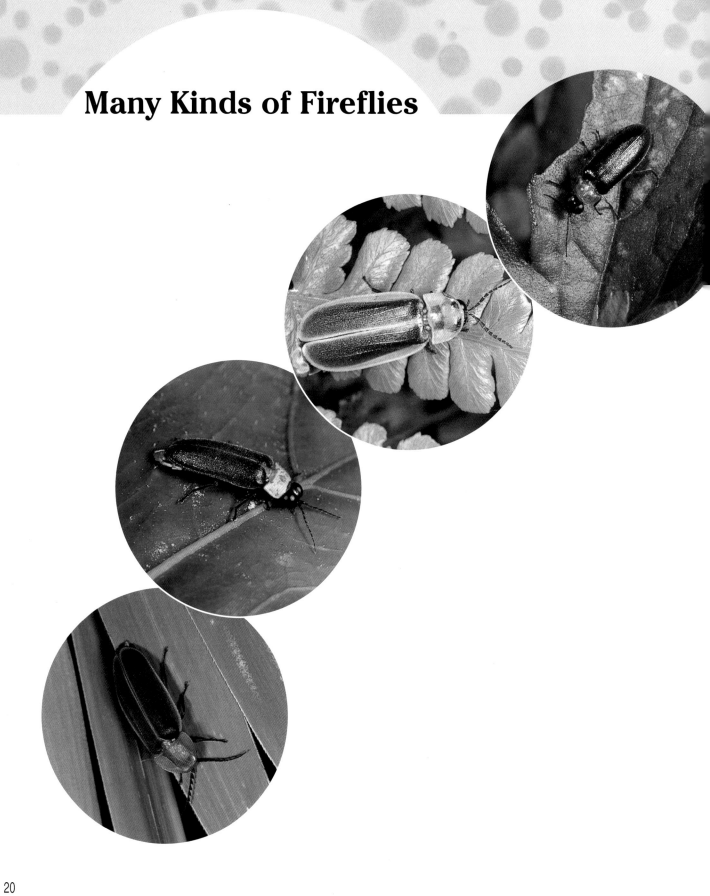

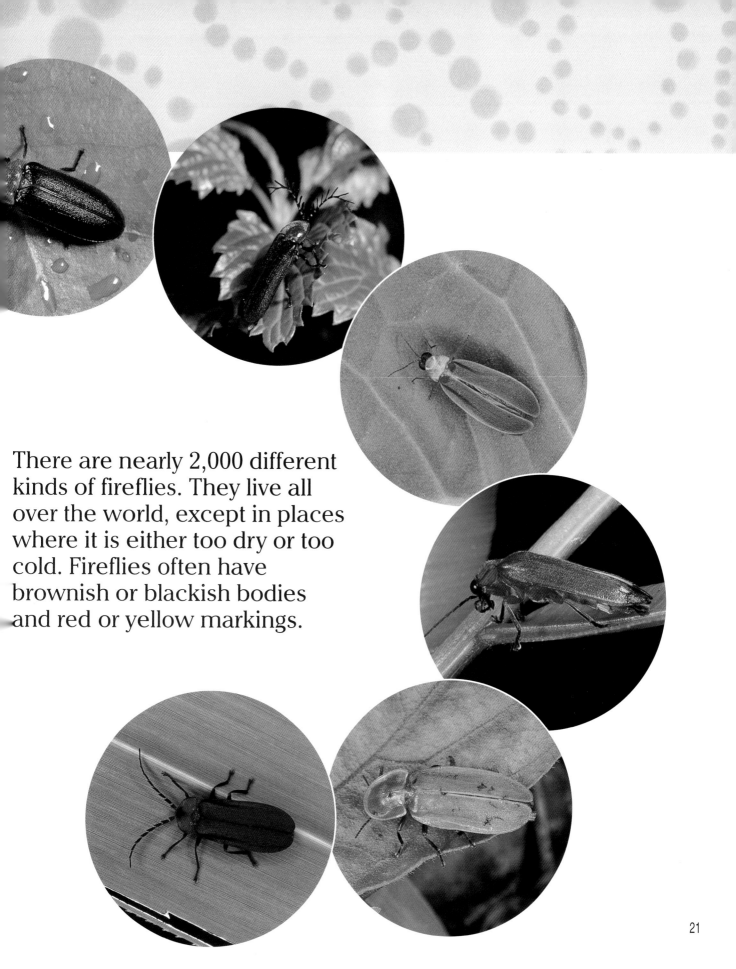

There are nearly 2,000 different kinds of fireflies. They live all over the world, except in places where it is either too dry or too cold. Fireflies often have brownish or blackish bodies and red or yellow markings.

Animals are not the only danger to fireflies. People hurt fireflies by taking over the areas where they live. Sprays used to kill some insect pests also end up killing fireflies. And bright outdoor lights make it hard to see these lightning bugs light.

But these unique insects live well in damp, peaceful spots around the world, as well as in crowded areas. So be on the lookout for their special flickering lights in your backyard!

For More Information

Coughlan, Cheryl. *Fireflies.* Mankato,
MN: Pebble Books, 2000.

St. Pierre, Stephanie. *Fireflies.* Crystal
Lake, IL: Heinemann Library, 2001.

Walker, Sally M. *Fireflies.* Minneapolis,
MN: Lerner, 2001.

Glossary

exoskeleton the hard covering on the
outside of an insect s body

larva the second stage in a firefly s life

molt to shed the outer skin or covering

pupa the third stage in a firefly s life

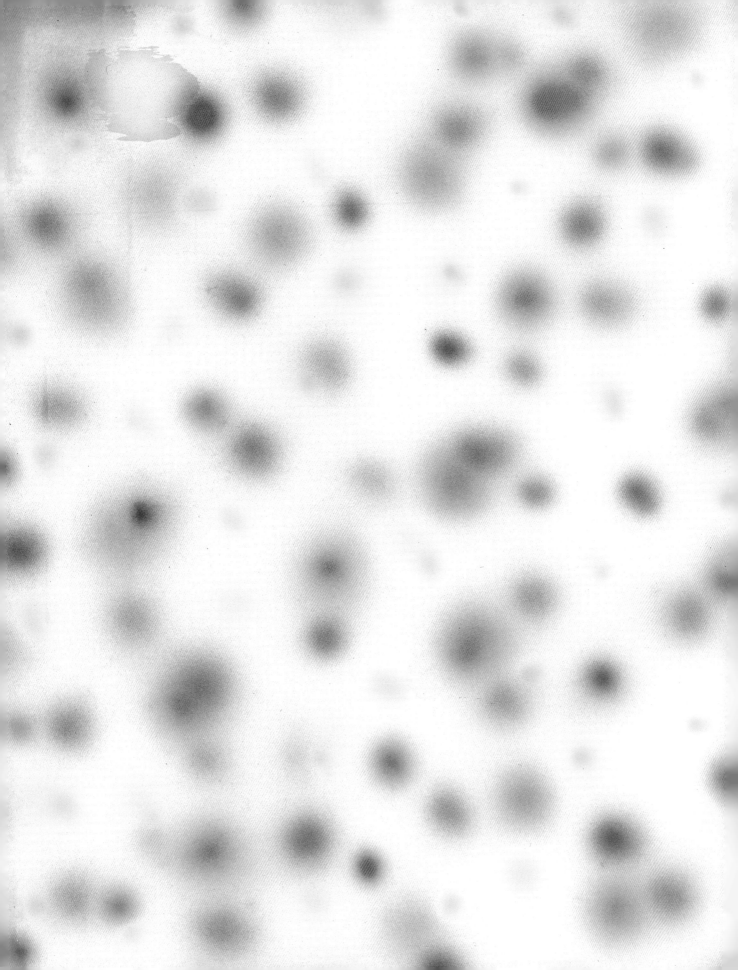